THE RIGHT WAY

TO DRAW

LANDSCAPES

To my long-suffering
companion and navigator.

THE RIGHT WAY TO

DRAW

LANDSCAPES

by

Mark Linley

PAPERFRONTS

Typeset in 10pt Times by One & A Half Graphics.
Printed and bound in Great Britain by Cox and Wyman Ltd., Reading, Berkshire.

The *Paperfronts* series and the *Right Way* series are both published by Elliot Right Way Books, Brighton Road, Lower Kingswood, Tadworth, Surrey, KT20 6TD, U.K.

CONTENTS

1

WE LOVE THE COUNTRYSIDE

This book is a complete course for beginner artists who want to learn how to draw landscape pictures. Step-by-step instructions are given for most of the drawings used as examples within these pages. You will start with easy-to-do studies which have been created to boost your self-confidence, and to show you that *anyone* can learn this skill. If you have never drawn anything except breath, don't worry; I have ways of teaching you!

At first glance the drawing used for figure 1 might seem difficult to do. Actually, this type of drawing is quite easy — once you have gained the necessary know-how about shading. By working through this book you will achieve a high standard of draftsmanship. You will feel justifiably pleased. Indeed, by purchasing this book you have already proved that you *want* to learn *The Right Way to Draw Landscapes*. So before you put pencil or pen to paper you are half way there. Well done!

People who want to draw landscapes tend to have a deep regard for our vanishing countryside. Naturally they wish to record what they see for posterity. It is my earnest hope that this book will help them. Personally, I have found that rambling and sketching combine well. There is no doubt that weekend rambling is an ever increasing popular activity which has particular appeal for artistic and 'green' people.

I love wild places and mountain scenes in particular. Originally I went in for mountain walking to overcome my

Fig. 1   Quite easy to draw.

nervousness of heights. This condition was cured in three days. Now, I enjoy a great sense of satisfaction and achievement when I stand on the summit of a mountain. I'm even tempted to shout skywards: "I'm on top of the world, Mother!" Such thoughts of high altitudes and breath-taking views made me spawn figure 2.

Figure 3 depicts a scene viewed from up on the Cuillin central ridge on the island of Skye. I discovered this panorama during what was, for me, the hardest, and most exciting of mountain walks yet undertaken. By the way, always walk with a friend, or a group. Mountains can be dangerous as well as beautiful.

Fig. 2   Peaks affect some of us in different ways.

Think success

If you have read my previous *Paperfront* books: *The Right Way to Draw,* or *The Right Way to Draw People,* then (hopefully!) you won't need any reminders about the way you should think. However, if you are a newcomer to my methods, then all that follows will be vital for your artistic success.

In art when we think '*I can*', so be it. We *really can*, because this is a positive thought which programmes every brain cell towards this end. Where so many people go wrong is that they allow self doubt to interfere. They worry about *whether* they can draw something, more than about *how* to do so. If you *think* you can't draw a landscape, you will be right; you will fail. This wrong instruction ("I can't") will be acted upon by your subconscious mind — your "computer" — just as quickly and as powerfully as when you have "I can" working for you. Unfortunately, many of us seem to be brain-washed to think negatively. Perhaps lack of encouragement during our school-days has resulted in what has become a bad habit. But habits can be changed! You just have to know that we all have unlimited potential. That means you, your grandmother, Uncle Ted, and me!

Fig. 3   On the Cuillin Ridge.

A true example of the power of turning negative into positive thought happened during an activity holiday which I was leading. A lady guest started off by saying frequently, "I can't draw". Sure enough, she couldn't. Her sketches were so bad that they were unrecognisable. I soon asked her to try a pencil study of some nearby plants. "Don't worry about failing. Just sit and look at them carefully. Then think to yourself 'I can do it'," I advised her, "and you will find that you can!". Two hours later she produced a really first-class drawing which I could hardly have bettered.

"I did what you said. I thought that I could draw them, and then I got on with it," she said happily. Positive thoughts do work fast. Hers is not an isolated story, as you may have guessed. The moral of it is that *you* can learn to draw easily. Never doubt it!

Teamwork

We shall work together through this book just as if you were in my student group. I will guide you, give you confidence, explain tricks of the trade as we go and, before you know it, you will draw attractive pictures. You may have a supportive spouse or a friend to encourage your efforts. However, if not, don't worry or allow non-artists to discourage you. You have me and my book to carry you forward.

Look

Being able to draw is not about handling a pen or pencil. That we can all do naturally. The big secret is to do with how you *look* at your subjects. When a sketch is wrong it is almost certainly because observation has been faulty. Your natural inclination may be to start drawing the moment you clap eyes on whatever you wish to sketch but it's a mistake. Take a long, careful look before making any marks on your pad. This simple step will dramatically cut down the number of errors you are likely to make. Although you must accept that making small blunders is part of the learning process and should be expected, generally, the longer you spend *looking* the better your pictures will be.

Beginner artists on their first attempt to draw a tree, for

example, tend to make the trunk and some branches quite straight, and the foliage into a round blob. A proper *look* would have shown them that a tree is anchored by roots which may be visible; that its leaves sprout from twigs; that the twigs grow from branches; and that these may divide as they come from the main trunk. A closer examination would also have revealed areas of deep shadow, and of reflected light. There's a lot we need to notice before we draw...

I will work on your powers of observation so that your skill and self-confidence can increase at your own pace.

What to use

Black-and-white drawings have a special charm and power. Indeed, before colour printing was invented, most illustrations were in this medium. Black ink and various nibs used to be common, but today artists use ready-made pens. All the drawings in this book were done with them. There is a huge range to choose from. I find that a small selection of pens, graded 0.1, 0.5, and 0.7, is more than adequate for most illustrations, and suggest that you purchase the same. Figure 4 will give you an idea of what to look for. Figure 5 shows examples of the widths of line different sizes of these pens produce. Despite being 'throw away' pens they are made to give long service. One pen will contain enough black ink to make dozens of drawings. And they are not expensive.

There is another type of pen which is also very useful for the artist who produces many drawings. This is a draftsman's pen. They come in many sizes and utilise an ink cartridge. Being technical pens they cost more, but with care will last for years. Both kinds are stocked by most good stationery and art material shops.

You will want to have a few soft pencils, 2B, 4B, or 6B, as well, because good pencil drawings of landscapes can be made. Also, all your early attempts should be lightly drawn in pencil first. A sharp blade is much better for keeping pencils in working order than a conventional sharpener. Artists cut a chisel point on their lead. This thin but wide point will draw fine or thick lines, making your pencil into a double-purpose one.

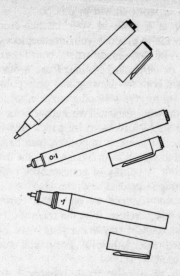

Fig. 4 Drawing pens.

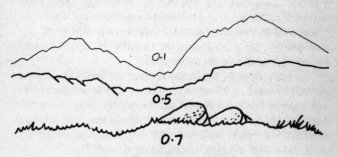

Fig. 5 Different line thicknesses.

A soft eraser is necessary. The person who makes no mistakes makes nothing! A medium-hard eraser will be handy for removing stubborn marks.

Having spoken of pencils I shall, however, concentrate more

on pen drawing so that ultimately you can copy, follow, and develop the sort of work shown in this book.

When you sit at a table in your kitchen-cum-studio, or wherever you decide to produce your masterpieces, a drawing board is useful. A purpose-made artists' board is expensive but strong plywood or chipboard is fine. I use a 50cm by 50cm piece of chipboard both for drawing and watercolour painting. One end I prop up to give a sloping surface, which helps the eye and makes drawing easier. Two hefty books do the job.

You will need an A4 size cartridge paper drawing pad, and a smaller A5 one for keeping in pocket, handbag, or car. An A5 pad was used to sketch from life many of the drawings used within these pages. A supply of good-quality typing paper is wonderful for rough sketches and can also be used for final work. This is far cheaper to buy than cartridge paper, especially when you purchase it by the ream (500 sheets), and so it provides an excellent way to cut your costs. For pen work a smooth surfaced paper is helpful. For pencil studies a rough surface can be used.

A good-quality small paint brush, number 3, 4, or 5, and a bottle of black drawing ink may be handy for blocking in large areas or for creating silhouettes. These last two items, however, are extras, and you can get by without them should you wish to hang on to your hard-earned money!

Some of the pictures in this book were drawn later, from photographs. On a hard walk, or in difficult, windy weather, a compact camera is therefore useful.

Generally, though, the outlay on gear for landscape drawing is much lower than for other art mediums. The satisfaction you will receive from this hobby will be worth many times more than the money spent. When your pictures reach an advanced standard you could well sell just one, and recover all your costs. Isn't that a happy, encouraging thought?

Important points
1. You CAN learn to draw.
2. Believe that you CAN.
3. Enjoy learning.
4. Don't expect perfection — for a chapter or two!

2

AN EASY START

All the drawings you do from this book should be bigger than the printed version. A larger drawing is usually easier to work on anyway. Use an A4 pad or typing paper for the following exercises. Begin with the very simple illustration in figure 6. This is called an extended landscape because it covers a large area of land. I happened upon this scene while on a ramble, and took a photograph of it from the vantage point of a hill top.

Draw figure 6 lightly in pencil. Leave a border round your work. This is a good habit to get into as it will give your sketches a professional look. You will probably find it helps if you start by drawing the outline rectangle inside which you wish to keep. Try working from top to bottom, as I do; it helps if you follow a methodical procedure.

Fill in the white paper

Illustrators and artists need to know how to fill a blank sheet of paper. This is done both with the lines of the drawing and with shading. The latter marks are used to suggest different forms, distance and so on. Use the most simple of shading for your first few exercises. Look at figure 7. Notice how distant patches of forest, hedges, and trees are recorded by vertical, even-spaced fine lines; how the field in the foreground is drawn with horizontal shading. Meadows further away are suggested by broken lines and small dashes. Trees in the foreground are made to look darker by a trick-of-the-trade often used, known as cross-hatching. Diagonal lines are

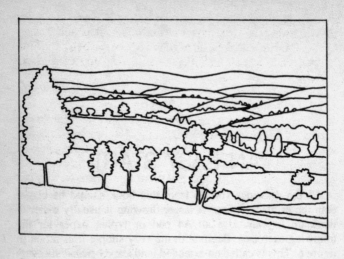

Fig. 6   An extended landscape.

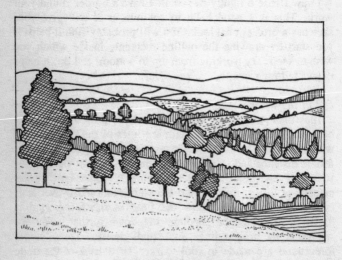

Fig. 7   Simple shading.

crossed at right-angles by similar diagonal lines going the opposite way. Grass is shown as little lines, dots and dashes. Go over your pencil out-line of figure 6/7 with a pen. Then rub out the pencil marks. Isn't it easy? You could do this with one eye closed!

Next, go to figure 8, which is a scene on the Isle of Wight. Take a long, careful *look* then draw in pencil.

Much of our U.K. countryside, incidentally, is inhabited by sheep. I always used to think of them as silly, nervous animals. However, when I was once sketching in the Yorkshire dales, an angry one with horns chased me. It must have gone mad. I finished up racing my friend to a stone stile where we climbed over to safety, but not before my friend had hurt her ankle. The sheep depicted in figure 8 are in the middle distance. They look like small oblongs with rounded ends. No detail is visible from a distance.

Figure 9 shows you how to shade in figure 8. Simplicity is the keynote again. However, the shading used for the trees in the foreground is slightly more advanced than in your previous sketch. Those trees to the left are partly cross-hatched, to help give a feeling of depth to the field. The ones in the middle are fully cross-hatched, with the addition of some simple squiggles. The effect of this extra shading is to bring these trees forward in the picture, towards your eye. Try it.

Simplification

Beginner artists tend to try to include every detail of what they see. This is impossible! Who has the time to spend a month drawing one tree? You can leave exact copying to a camera. What you must aim to do is simplify what you want to draw. Indeed, one of the highest forms of art is that in which detail is left out, the artist suggesting what things are like with as few lines as possible. You have a lot of freedom. You can remove unwanted trees or buildings, change the way a river runs, or put in features that will improve a picture.

You are learning step-by-step the quickest way to reach a very high level of skill. Don't try too hard to produce identical copies of my drawings. That is not important at this stage. I want you to develop your own style. You can use your own

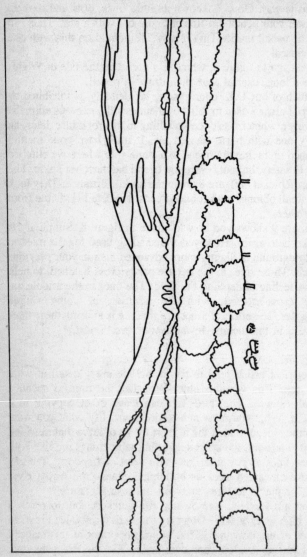

Fig. 8 Isle of Wight scene.

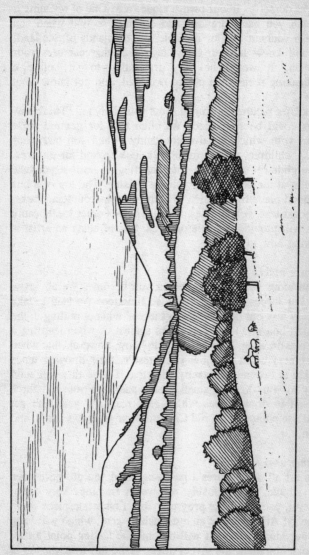

Fig. 9 More advanced shading.

ideas about how to create shading. We are all different, and express ourselves in our own, unique, way. One of my aims is to teach you basic drawing and shading, so that when you unleash yourself on, for example, the highlands of Scotland, you will know how to draw any scene that captures your attention. It would be very frustrating to sit before a breathtaking scene, pen poised over pad, and not know what to do!

Look for pictures as you go about your daily toil. Think how things could be simplified. We often take for granted those scenes with which we live constantly. When you take your spouse, children, or dog for a walk look around for pictures. If you glide off to work in your chauffeured Rolls-Royce take a squint at the countryside you are passing. The top of a bus is a good place from which to scan your environment. Parks, pretty gardens, golf courses, and all kinds of other local beauty spots will provide possible pictures. Part of being an artist is knowing how to *look*.

Practice makes perfect

The more you draw the better you become. We all know that, but success requires self-discipline too! We tend to take the easy way out (and expect to succeed without putting in the drawing hours ...) but this works against us when learning a skill like drawing. It's interesting to know, however, that when newcomers begin to show good results their drawing tends quickly to become pleasantly addictive. I hope this will soon apply to you. Keep a small sketch pad with you and force yourself to draw scenes within easy reach. If you can't get about use photographs, old Christmas, or greetings cards, and so on.

Another step forward

So far all the pictures I have suggested you do, have been very simple, and probably not worth framing. Very soon, however, you will make progress. Your first masterpiece is not far away! Aim to create an eye-catching gem, which will hang on your kitchen wall. It will become the talking point for all visitors. You know the sort of thing: "I did this from the top of

Fig. 10   A roadside sketch.

Snowdon. We went there to exercise my bad leg but I couldn't resist dashing off a quickie of the wonderful scene below me!"

Next step ahead

Figure 10 is an outline sketch, drawn from a roadside in Scotland. Draw this either straight off with a pen, or lightly in pencil. Figure 11 is the same scene shaded and completed. Notice how thin, close lines are used to break up the white area of the sky. Leaves are suggested on the near trees, then lightly shaded over by diagonal lines. A few extra lines denote clefts in the rock in the foreground. The lines used for grass are more detailed near the artist, but they fade into dots and dashes further away. Now finish your picture in a similar fashion.

The final illustration in this chapter, figure 12, is the most advanced one in this section. It has been drawn in stages. Figures 13 and 14 show how you *must* set the scene with the outlines before you can tackle the detail. They should make it simple for you to copy figure 12. What more could you want? A drink? Very well then, but don't hang about too long; we have a lot to do!

Fig. 11 Shaded in.

Making a landscape drawing is a construction job. Different parts may be put together, but all sketches are built. Examine figure 12. Then start to copy this as in figure 13 — which is stage one of this construction. Use a size 0.5 pen to draw the mountains, near the river bank, and the large rocks. Notice how much blank paper there is to fill as you define your outlines.

Stage two, in figure 14, shows how a little more major detail is added. Now you have a few ripples to indicate water, broken outlines of trees in the foothills and more detail in the boulders and the single fir tree. Put the changes in with the same pen.

Return to figure 12 to complete the sketch. Change to your size 0.1 pen. Draw the sky lines first, then the distant trees and the shading on the hills. Your next task is to shade in the middle banks, followed by the boulders. Fine cracks on the rocks and the small wavy lines in the water are the last for you to tackle. You have now finished your most advanced picture. Congratulations! You are on your way.

Shading, with a little practice, should be done rapidly. To go fast is better. It helps to cut down errors because there isn't time to worry about, or doubt, your ability. Just allow your

Fig. 12 A slightly more advanced drawing.

computer (brain) to work for you. Be bold and confident. Ignore minor mistakes; indeed, expect them and take them in your stride.

By now you will know that ink illustrations take time and

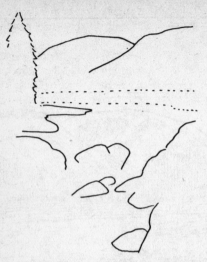

Fig. 13   The basic construction.

Fig. 14   A little more added.

patience rather than a great talent. Artists find time to improve their crafts. I am sure you will do the same now you have joined our ranks.

By the way, there are as many, if not more, winter scenes drawn by artists as there are produced in other seasons. I think the countryside is special at any time, but — please forgive my bias — I must admit that sketching in warm sunshine beats standing knee-deep in slush in an icy force ten gale!

Important points
1. Be confident and bold.
2. *Look* and *look* again.
3. Be pleased with your progress.

3

DON'T RUSH YOUR BRIDGES

Bridges are a common feature of our countryside, and they are often used by artists as the centre-piece of a landscape picture. I shall show you how to obtain the effect of rock and stone, and give you an idea of how a bridge is constructed. Whenever you come across a nice looking bridge don't rush across it.

Loiter with intent

Walk around, under, and over the bridge. Try to fathom how the builders put it together. Did they use local materials? Is it an ancient structure? Who uses it? Would it make a good picture?

Examine figure 16. The top sketch is of a bridge in the Yorkshire Dales. Large slabs of local stone were used for the central arch. Stone and rocks, set in mortar, form the sides and are topped by big ridge stones. In this illustration each stone has been separately drawn. Notice how the builders used large rocks as part of the base, and thin ones around the arch. It's easy to draw. Have a shot at it.

The middle illustration is of a quite different structure. This is a fairly new bridge on the Linn of Dee, Scotland. When I visited this beautiful place I was impressed by the way designers had come up with a modern idea which fitted into the surroundings so well. Natural rock was used for the buttresses of the bridge and perfectly cut rectangular stones for the sides.

Copy this sketch. You have to pre-draw the straight lines in pencil with a rule. Small dots and dashes suggest the texture of rock.

Fig. 16   Different structures.

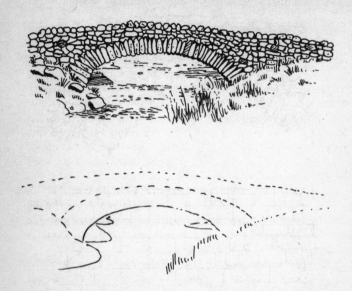

Fig. 17 The ancient pack-horse bridge at Wantendlath.

The bottom drawing is of an ancient pack-horse bridge. There are still many of these lovely relics in our countryside. This bridge is an example of wonderful craftsmanship. See how tightly each rock fits into the whole design. No mortar was used. It's rather like dry stone walling in construction. The men who built it must have had a talent for jig-saw puzzles!

A tip worth remembering, when drawing walls, bridges, and some buildings, is that it isn't necessary exactly to copy each individual rock or stone. This would take ages to do. Although each piece will need to be drawn individually, the best way is to decide what shapes the material has, and then draw *similar* shapes. In this bridge you can see that tooth-like rocks were used for the arch, while many different-sized stones went into the sides.

A 0.1 size pen was used for these illustrations. Now you can try them. Draw each stone and rock separately. Put in a few cracks and lines, and there you are — finished. Wasn't it easy?

Your first little gem

I have used Wantendlath bridge for figure 17. This old pack-horse bridge straddles a stream which comes from a tarn at the foot of impressive hills. Wantendlath is a hamlet of small cottages, and farm buildings, which nestle between steep rocky mountains. I drew the structure with no background detail. One very hot summer day I sat on a large boulder to draw this picture. A pony took an interest in the event. He was feeling peckish, and raided my bag for salad sandwiches and an apple. (Figure 18). All was not lost though! There was a tea shop handy so it was my lucky day!

Look at the lower sketch in figure 17; then copy this in pencil. When you are satisfied with your outlines, complete the drawing with a 0.1 size pen to match the top illustration. See how stones, grass, and water have been suggested. There is nothing too difficult for you to manage.

The next sketch of the same bridge was taken from the opposite side for figure 19. Now it's time for you to create your

Fig. 18 A peckish pony.

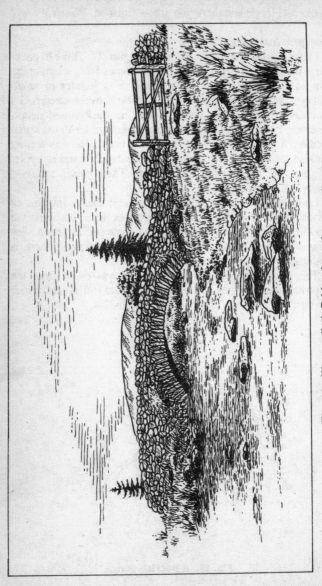

Fig. 19 Wantendlath Bridge from the opposite side.

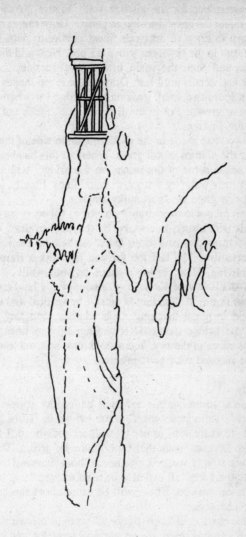

Fig. 20 Start with a pencil sketch.

first masterpiece for the kitchen wall. Figure 20 shows you how to make the basic drawing in pencil. Once this is right you can begin to draw in ink your finest picture to date.

First, put in the sky lines with a 0.1 pen. Next add the distant hill line and then the main bridge construction. Leave all shading and details until last. Draw in the stone shapes one-by-one, but leave two small gaps on the bridge for where tufts of grass have grown. Put in the five bar gate. Flesh out, almost black, the fir trees.

Now you can shade in the rocks, the underside of the bridge, and add the clumps of tall grass. When all this has been done, lightly shade some of the stones on the bridge, with diagonal lines. Portray water by wavy horizontal lines. Finally, jot down some more grass by short spiky strokes.

Be careful not to over-draw by trying to fill every bit of blank space. It isn't always necessary, by the way, to draw edge-to-edge. Pictures that have been faded out around the sides look quite attractive. The last job for you is to ink a frame round your drawing. Now choose a space on your wall!

As a small reward for your efforts copy the landscape with bridge in figure 21. Shading is mostly by vertical and diagonal lines and by cross-hatching. Dots, dashes, and tiny oblongs record the bridge material. Radiating, broken lines give an effect of space in the sky. You should have no trouble with this one. Be pleased with your progress.

Be dotty

A useful technique for artists is called dot stipple. I have used this on the stone work on the bridge in figure 22. This ancient structure, still in use by walkers and sheep, I found in the Lake District — another super place for artists. The heavy stones are simply wedged together without mortar. Dot stipple suggests their form. It can also be used for depicting trees and many other subjects. There will be more about the technique in later chapters.

Take a challenge! Copy figure 22 straight off with your 0.1 size pen. Again, there are no big problems for you here.

Remember, the more you draw, the better and quicker you become. Before pressing on try the following quiz.

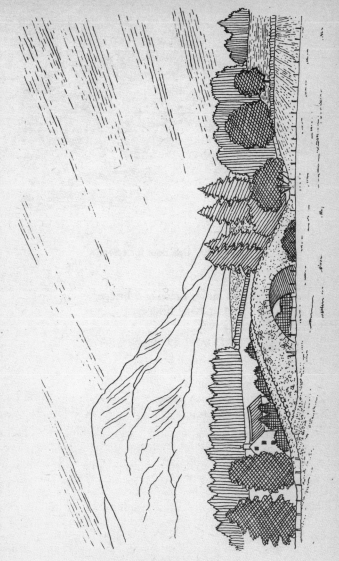

Fig. 21 Landscape with bridge.

Fig. 22   Use dots for effect.

Quiz
1. How would you tackle drawing a bridge?
2. Give a tip about drawing bridges.
3. How is grass shown?
4. What technique is good for rough stone?

Answers
1. Study it from *all* angles.
2. Don't try to draw each stone.
3. By short lines or dashes.
4. Dot stipple.

4

TANGLE WITH TIMBER

Today, perhaps more than ever before, we have discovered how important trees are to life on our planet. Trees provide food, medicine, organic material for the soil, oxygen for the atmosphere. They prevent erosion, give shelter, balance nature, and can transform a barren area. Each mature tree is a wild-life city. Birds, animals and insects abound. When chopped down — in minutes with a chain saw — the timber has many uses.

Trees are a joy to our eyes and they refresh our spirits. When I visit my favourite forest, the Wyre, to the surprise of any companion who might be with me, I talk to the trees. "Hello! It's nice to see you again," I say. My enthusiasm for trees, wild places and creatures dates from childhood. I like to feel that I can be part of the scene when I am let loose!

Get to know trees

The more you know about the subjects that you want to draw, the easier it is for you to refine the detail. As you can guess, it boils down to having a good *look* first. So far you have drawn trees in a simple way. Now I shall show you how to depict trees with added realism. In many landscape pictures trees tend to be in the middle or far distance. They can be handled on the simple lines learned hitherto. However, where a tree is the main foreground subject in an illustration, then in order to draw it accurately you need to know how to obtain the detailed effects of bark, branches, and foliage.

What problems must you solve? First ask yourself what shape the tree is. Is it round, tall, or spread out? What do the

Fig. 23 How to suggest foliage.

leaves look like? Are they fine, broad, pointed, or odd shaped? What is the bark like? Smooth, craggy, ridged, ringed, or what? As with all subjects, it is essential constantly to re-examine the construction of the items that go into a picture.

Figure 23 illustrates how to depict foliage, trunk, and

branches. Notice how dark shadows help to give the trees depth and form. The top drawing, a maple tree, has been shaded on one side and almost blocked out where the deep shadows are. A few small, fine pen strokes were used to suggest the grain of the bark.

The two trees in the middle were shaded after they were drawn, with light, short strokes. These were cross-hatched to give deep shadows.

The bottom sketches were deliberately enlarged to show you how to make your foliage.

Copy all these trees in pencil. Then go over your work with a size 0.1 pen. There are no great difficulties for you. You don't have to use the identical shapes or shading which I have used. You may prefer to express your own ideas of how to obtain similar results. You could easily become the best tree artist in the whole world. I hope that you do!

Control your scribble

Figure 24 is comprised of a variety of trees and bushes drawn in the same manner experienced artists would use on work to be published or exhibited. How is it done? Answer, very easily! The effect of leaves and shadows to make up the sort of tree drawn in figure 24 is created by what I call a controlled scribble. *After* the main tree shape has been drawn with fine, dotted pencil lines (later to be erased), this outline is then filled by controlled scribble. Hold your pen fairly loosely. Obtain the desired effect by making quick, small twirls, circles, squiggles, wiggles, dots and dashes. Produce deep, dark shadows with white bits showing through to give a sense of texture and form. With just a little practice it really is easy to do. The finished result is very professional. Now try your own scribble!

Winter trees

After the leaves have fallen in winter, we can clearly see how a tree is constructed, and how one differs from another. Look at the elm, at the top of figure 25. See how different it is from the poplar, birch and fir on the same page. Patience and good observation are required to draw a winter tree accurately. Once

Fig. 24   A controlled scribble.

again you must ask yourself exactly what it is you see. What shape is the tree or bush? Which way do its branches grow — up, out, or down? What are the twigs like? How does the bark appear — ridged, wrinkled, or smooth?

The best way to start your drawing of a winter tree is with

an outline shape. I then move to the trunk, follow by putting in main branches and, last of all, add the twigs. The only problem with this kind of picture is that it takes time, but any attractive drawing is well worth a small slice of our precious life. Besides, it keeps us off the streets!

Trees to the front

Artists frequently use trees as a focal point in a picture. Figure 26 shows how a group of fir trees on an island has been used in the foreground to give an idea of the scale of the mountains beyond. Copy this drawing. Start with the sky lines to suggest cloud movement there, then sketch in the hills, followed by the island and the tall trees. The band of middle-distance trees is portrayed with a controlled scribble. The same technique is applied to the bushes on the island. The fir branches are suggested by masses of two, three or four short strokes drawn with a fine pen. Notice how some of these point upwards, while others go downwards. The portrayal of water is obtained by wavy, horizontal dashes as in previous work. This little picture could be another one for your kitchen wall. If, by some remote chance, your masterpiece isn't quite up to your expectations give it away to someone you don't much like!

How is your bark?

For a good tree to be featured as the main subject of a picture you must know how to produce realistic looking bark. Figure 27, drawn in one of my local parks, shows four types of bark. The beautiful silver birch tree is a popular subject for landscape work, and is simple to draw. See how the white trunk is marred by triangular black blotches which increase in number towards the base of the tree. The bark surface pattern is shown by curved lines which run around the trunk. The branches are dark in tone and this is shown by shading.

The trunk of a fir tree is quite different. The bark is made up of large over-lapping scales which appear to hang down the tree. Each of these slate-like pieces, when viewed close up, can be seen to have small flakes in its make up. I have depicted them with a few fine lines.

The common oak, often drawn or painted by artists, is nice

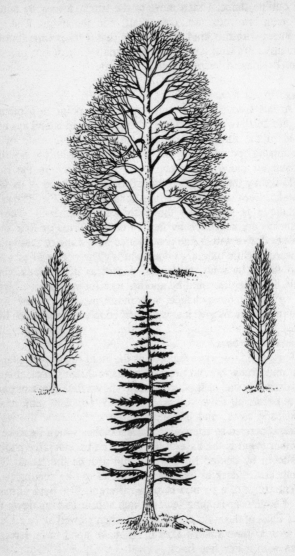

Fig. 25 Trees in winter.

Fig. 26   Trees in the foreground.

to sketch. The bark is composed of rough, deep ridges, with many cracks and crannies. These trees have heavy, sometimes twisted, branches.

A point to remember, with trees, is to draw one side in shadow, with markings more detailed than the opposite side. This helps to create depth and shape. If you use the same way of depicting bark for the whole trunk, it will look flat. Make one side lighter, with less detail.

The beech tree is another common tree which is fine to draw. The bark lines go around the trunk and are smooth compared to those of the oak.

See how the roots are suggested on the different trees in figure 27.

Copy all the drawings straight off with a size 0.1 pen.

Go behind the bushes

It pays to spend a bit of time behind the bushes, in the name of art of course! Figure 28 illustrates how bushes and small

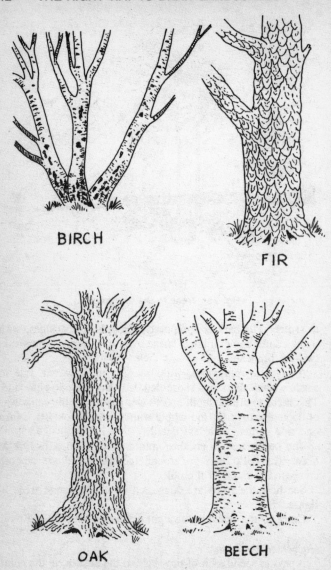

BIRCH

FIR

OAK

BEECH

Fig. 27   Tree trunk detail.

Fig. 28 Scribbled bushes.

shrubs are drawn. Well executed, they are attractive parts of a picture. Notice how the scribbled dense shadows tend to project the lighter parts and this helps to suggest the form of a bush. Trunks and branches are only partly seen. Copy the examples in figure 28. Doing them will give you more practice with your scribble.

Assignments
1. Draw your nearest tree.
2. Draw the trunks of four different trees.
3. Look at some bushes and then draw them with a controlled scribble.
4. Examine the foliage of a tree in the distance. Then draw the tree.

5

TAKE TO THE HILLS

You should have gained some skill in sketching rocks and stone in chapter 3, Don't Rush Your Bridges. Your experience will now be extended. I will show you how to draw the huge boulders and rocks which feature in many mountain scenes.

The island of Skye, for me, has the most wonderful mountain range in our country. The Lake District and the Scottish Highlands come a close equal second. I will, however, for this chapter take you, via sketches, mainly on a visit to one of the majestic peaks of the Black Cuillin mountains of Skye. My drawings began on a visit when I once clambered up there on a hot summer day.

Rocks and boulders simply drawn.

Take a look at figure 29. The top illustration is of a cairn which is a heap of stones made to way-mark mountain walks. (They may have been used for other purposes in years past.) This particular one was in the Lake District. Notice the vertical lines and the cross-hatching used to depict shadow. The middle drawing shows boulders drawn very simply. Fine lines suggest cracks, splits and texture. The bottom sketch is of rock slabs with small ridges and cracks. Heavy infilling is used for the darkest parts. These are all easy drawing jobs. Copy them all. Then move on to figure 30.

The new technique here is one for shading clouds. They are best outlined lightly in pencil; then you use a pen to put in the sky lines round the fluffy shapes; finally you erase the pencil outlines. Go on to shade your mountain. Use cross-hatching to

Fig. 29   Rocks and boulders – simply drawn.

Fig. 30   An easy exercise.

make deep shadow. The rocks in the foreground show well in contrast to the mountains beyond. I'm sure you will find this another easy exercise to do.

Figure 31 takes you a step further on. It has a similar cloud and sky effect, but the mountains contain slightly more shading than those in previous sketches. Lots of little lines were used in a kind of controlled scribble. The sea is suggested by horizontal lines. The reflection of the lowest hill, nearest the sea, is depicted by wavy ones. Copy this picture.

Figure 32 has dark-looking mountains which are easy to draw. The dense areas were obtained with cross-hatching. After sketching this example in ink, you may care to draw it again in pencil or using a coloured crayon. It is useful to increase the range of your artistic skill. Each medium brings a different majesty to the picture. Try them and see!

Interesting rock structures

On a walk on the Island of Skye I came across a beautiful bay. Seals swam in sparkling blue water; sea-birds filled the air with their cries. The rock formation in the bay, shown in figure 33, was fascinating. I climbed up onto the shelf-like part, but could go no higher without a rope or a helper. The rock structure was buff-coloured, and it had several kinds of texture. There were slabs, boulders, splits, and pebble size projections, all of which were hard on hands, knees and shins.

Figure 34 is of the basic shape of this ancient natural architecture. Draw the outline in pencil then proceed in ink as in figure 33. This illustration took me around an hour to complete after I had the outline in place. I started with the sky lines, then moved on to the dot stipple on the high point of

Fig. 31 Lots of little lines used.

Fig. 32 An easily drawn dark mountain range.

the rock. I worked slowly down to the deep shadow under the shelf, and then suggested with fine lines the lava layers in the base. There are no great difficulties. Just take your time. Your copy will be one to treasure.

A trip to the top

The remaining drawings in this chapter illustrate my trip to the top of Sgurr Alasdair, which is a naked rock pinnacle on the central ridge of the Cuillin mountains on Skye. I was a novice hill-walker then but had the good fortune to be escorted by a superb leader who prompted me to try to become a good all-round rambler. If you ever attempt this walk be sure to allow the best part of a day for it. The going is hard and mostly uphill over varied terrain.

Figure 35 shows part of the region along the way. The distant peaks were the object of my journey. The ground was littered with huge slabs between which tough clumps of red grass grew. I used a size 0.1 pen to draw this. Draw your version of it. If you decide to scale it up a much larger size than in this book use a size 0.5 pen.

Fig. 33 An interesting structure.

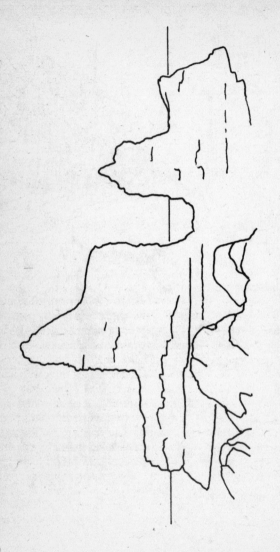

Fig. 34 Draw the basic shapes first.

Fig. 35   A varied terrain.

Awe-inspiring peaks

After an arduous slog of several miles on from the place shown in figure 35, I reached the spectacular scene portrayed in figure 36. The track led steeply down to the base of Alasdair. To give you an idea of the immense size of its awe-inspiring peaks I have put two figures in. The small boulders higher up, recorded by dots, were knee high! The larger ones were taller than a house, with the odd one as high as a cathedral!

The white path in the centre of the picture is called the Great Stone Chute which is a very apt name for it. Highly experienced mountaineers (and a few foolhardy novices like me) use this to descend quickly. The idea is to make a dash for it over the stony surface. This causes a carpet of quite large stones to propel you onwards. You feel as if you are being whisked down with the speed of an express train. Having a crack at it was one of the most exciting experiences of my life. I have heard that the record time taken for this very steep drop is eleven seconds. This feat I can assure you is hardly one challenged by the sane!

The route to the top is to the left of the chute. Many of the boulders are too big to climb over, so the going is slow. However, the views from the top are truly magnificent and worth all the hard effort.

For *your* hardest challenge to date draw this scene. It's much easier to sketch than it is to climb! Be prepared to spend two hours or more on this picture. Start with a pencil drawing. Then just keep plugging away. I shall leave you to examine the drawing and work out how I have done the shading as part of your study of how to portray mountainous terrain. If your attention does flag stop for a break. Stroke your cat, dog, or spouse. Have a coffee. Then resume your masterpiece for the lounge wall.

On top of the world

A view from the top of the Cuillin ridge is featured in figure 37. The dark grey peaks stood out against a shining sea and a

Fig. 36   Awe-inspiring peaks.

Fig. 37 A view from the top of Alasdair.

blue sky. Distant shore and island disappeared into a heat haze. Can you guess what I shouted when I stood on the summit? After the last exercise, drawing this illustration will be child's play for you. You could then try copying figures 1 and 3 in chapter 1 just for fun!

Quiz
1. What is the best way to fill in deep shadow?
2. What is infilling useful for?
3. What would you use dot stipple for?
4. Fine lines are good for what?

Answers
1. Cross-hatching or heavy infilling.
2. Trees, bushes, vegetation, distant mountains, rocks.
3. Stone, trees, bushes, rocks, and many other subjects.
4. Fine details of all kinds.

6

BUILDINGS IN LANDSCAPES

Self-discipline

Different artists have different pet subjects. It could be that you don't have much enthusiasm for drawing buildings, but it is important to be self-disciplined in order to become skilled. To want to devote all your attention to your chosen subject is quite natural. This, however, tends to work against you in the long term. I state this from experience. For years I put my energy into becoming a reasonably good wildlife artist to the exclusion of other subjects. The net result was that, although my animals and birds were quite good, the backgrounds to my pictures were not of an equal standard. My people drawings in the early years also left a lot to be desired.

It pays to tackle all subjects in a professional way. The skill required, for example, to draw buildings accurately is just the same as that needed for drawing trees, animals, people, or whatever. All problems of draftsmanship are related. It is only the way we think about them that varies.

I have had students who, at first, shunned drawing a certain subject, only to find out after trying, that what was feared proved to be that at which they were best! Learn to draw *everything* well. Then you can specialise...

Start with basic construction lines

You are about to learn how to draw some of the buildings which crop up in landscapes. At this point in the book I won't worry you about the theories of perspective. There will be more about them in a later chapter. Obtaining the correct angle

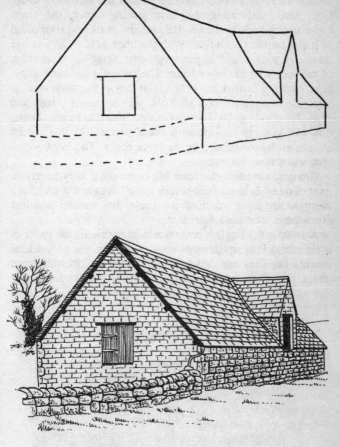

Fig. 38 An old farm building.

of slope in a roof, or the slanting lines of a building, is mostly
a matter of good observation to experienced artists. You will
learn to apply such experience as you progress.

The old barn used for figure 38 is in Northamptonshire. The
way that the big stones had been used in the low wall and sides

interested me. The end walls of red brick contrasted with the natural material. I wondered if the builder had run out of stone. Copy this illustration by first putting down the main construction lines as shown. Position this book and your piece of paper beside each other. With the book held steady in one hand, lay your pencil or pen lengthwise along the main ridge of the roof with the other hand. Then transfer the same angle your drawing instrument is laying at across the book over to your piece of paper. Just shift the pen or pencil across and draw. Do the same for the other angled lines and slopes. Doing this will give you information about perspective. I used dot stipple to denote texture in the large rocks. The ivy-covered tree was added for interest.

Drawing sloping lines from life correctly is very nearly as easy. Simply hold up your pen or pencil between you and the line you are after, matching the angle, and transfer that line down onto your masterpiece.

A walk in the English countryside often reveals the tower of a church poking up through trees. Churches are very useful landmarks. They are shown on all good maps. Ramblers can check that their walk is on course by correctly locating a

Fig. 39   Clapham Church (Yorkshire).

Fig. 40   Ruins are easy to draw.

church. Old churches are especially nice to draw. Look at figure 39. Draw this and note how one side of the building has been shaded. The humble dot and dash is a wonderful device for artists. Here, they achieve the impression of stone, with ease. You will see that the trees and bushes were drawn using the same technique described in chapter 4. This church should be easy for you to copy.

Old ruins are simple to draw and quite interesting to see. The heap of rocks in figure 40 is all that remains of a castle in the Yorkshire Dales. Sheep follow everywhere; I put in two to give a sense of scale. A copy of this example should take about half an hour. Off you go!

Variety is good

There are many types of building scattered around our countryside. The ones that are totally different from modern

Fig. 41 A windmill that is easy to draw.

dwellings are often the most interesting for us to sketch. Windmills, for instance, are not normally found next to the supermarket in the high street! Flat country such as in Holland, or the English Fens, is a better place to look for them. Figure 41 shows the way a windmill can dominate land it stands on. This particular specimen is both round and tapered. Draw the outline in pencil first. Make sure your basic lines are right before completing it in ink.

Figure 42 gives an example of a mill in the Cotswolds at a place called Lower Slaughter. How did it get a name like that? There is a resident artist in this hamlet who earns his living by producing paintings of the beautiful cottages found there. Good luck to him! I should like you to draw the mill in figure 42. There is slightly more to this one, but nothing beyond your powers. Start with a pencil sketch of the main building. Put in an outline of the mill wheel, the stone wall and the shed. Make sure you are happy with the overall proportions before you turn to ink. Notice the way the roofs come together, and how the wheel has been treated. The stone work, trees, grass and water are drawn as in other exercises you have already successfully done. I have deliberately left out both sky lines and clouds. I want you to do them in your own way. Your finished picture may merit a frame; it's up to you.

I visited another hamlet to draw the building in figure 43.

Fig. 42 A Cotswold mill and stream.

Fig. 43   A stone-built old building.

This one is in the Lake District. I am not sure if it was once
a barn, stable or cottage. The dark grey stone used in the
construction seemed to me to be the same as that seen in the
hills overlooking this scene. I drew the stones separately. Then
I shaded with diagonal lines over the ones drawn in the end
wall. This gives shadow and so suggests depth. The shrubs and
the tree were produced with a controlled scribble. Draw this
and pop in a few clouds just for practice.

Farm buildings

Modern farms with water towers, stock sheds and massive
barns are not always very pleasant to see. Many old farms are
also spoilt for the viewer by rusty sheds and black-painted
corrugated sheet barns. There are, however, still a few

traditional farms about. I found the one shown in figure 44 up in the Yorkshire Dales. I sat on a plastic bag to draw this lovely scene. I did not include a pile of rocks and an unsightly shed in my picture. My original sketch was only 13cm across. I used a size 0.1 pen. The dry stone wall in the foreground was made up with many different sized stones of various shades. The wooden gate just about hung together and it tilted at an angle to the wall. The house was small with white-painted walls. There were tall clumps of reddish grass sprouting from the swampy ground and, of course, the "inevitable" sheep. The distant hills and patchwork of fields gave a sense of space and freedom. Copy this illustration.

Figure 45 shows farm buildings set against a background of hills. Dot stipple seemed the obvious way to suggest the large areas of scree (loose stones). Draw this example; it could be

Fig. 44 A Yorkshire hill farm.

another little gem for your hall, along with the sheep shelter and bridge shown in figure 46. The latter small drawing is a good example of dot stipple work.

In Wales and Scotland you sometimes come across a stone built cottage of the sort illustrated in figure 47. I expect these picturesque dwellings are hard to live in if you are used to the creature-comforts of a town house. They are, however, a delightful feature for the landscape artist. A cottage set against a background of impressive hills like the example in figure 47 should by now be straightforward for you to copy.

Fig. 45   A farm in the hills.

Fig. 46 Sheep shelter and bridge.

Thatched cottages

Many people dream of owning a thatched cottage. These old buildings are part of our English heritage. They are lovely to look at, though I suspect not necessarily very practical to live in! There are several ways of drawing thatch. I prefer to create the image with tiny dashes which follow the slope of the roof. You cannot attempt to draw individual reeds. The result would be a mess! Notice in figure 48 how I have left areas of light to highlight the thatch. Copy this cottage.

Quiz

1. What is your first task in drawing a landscape?
2. How should you start?
3. What is the main problem in drawing buildings?
4. Which drawing techniques are useful for them?

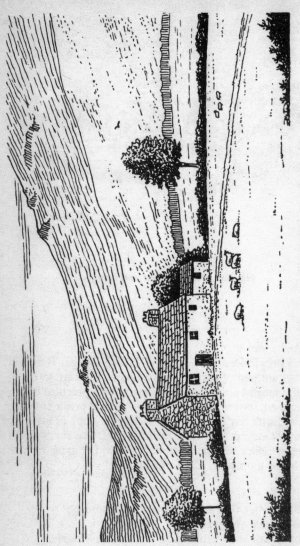

Fig. 47 A farm cottage in the hills.

Fig. 48 How to draw the thatch.

Answers
1. Take a long, good *look*.
2. With a basic outline sketch.
3. Getting the slopes right (perspective).
4. Dots and dashes, controlled scribble, fine lines, shading.

7

OFF TO THE SEASIDE

You deserve a nice break! So, in this chapter, we are off to the seaside. You may, like me, enjoy a spot of beachcombing or a romp along windswept shores. Some folk find their idea of heaven on a crowded beach but the reverse is true for me and, I suspect, for most artists; our joy is to sketch rolling waves, sunny sands or majestic cliffs.

After all your practice on landscapes, you already have the ability to draw a good seascape! The techniques for your pen are essentially the same.

Look for light and dark

An attractive seashore scene may, at first glance, seem to contain very little. Figure 50 is an example. There are two jagged rocks, a line of distant cliffs and a few gulls. Breakers with ever decreasing waves lap over wet sand which reflects the rock shapes. There is a pale sun which sets off an unusual pattern of clouds.

Drawing this picture was quite easy. I began with a line for the horizon and then put in the rocks. I gave these substance by using plenty of cross-hatching but I was careful to leave the rock edges bare. This was to show where sunlight was reflected. Waves and breakers I formed by using different thicknesses of line. I made extensive use of wavy lines, dashes, and dots, and created seaweed with a controlled scribble.

Your one new problem with this drawing might be the gulls. Look carefully at these. Note the rough oval shape of the body with a neck that can stretch or contract. The beak is short and

Fig. 50 Not much to see – at first glance.

Fig. 51 A solitary figure on a shore.

slightly curved at the tip. The eyes are set fairly high in the head. I used light shading to distinguish the grey wings and the back of the birds in the sun. See where the light and dark areas are. But note the different treatment of the birds in the shadow of the rock. Now copy this illustration with a size 0.1 pen.

The methods for figure 50 apply equally to figure 51, a solitary figure on a shore. I drew this human quite simply. Figures of this kind are often used to add a little interest to pictures. They don't need much detail. I included the girl to give an impression of freedom, and space. Notice the way she walks into the scene rather than out of it. This is an important composition point. You want your viewer to look into and around your masterpieces, so design them with this in mind. I will return to this aspect later on.

If you have no experience at figure drawing try a few quick pencil sketches before you start with pen work. Then have a go at this illustration.

Learn from the masters

We can all learn from master-artists, both past and present. We can study their work and try to fathom how they achieved different effects. Sometimes we are even lucky enough to visit the places and look for ourselves at the scenes which were the subjects of their drawings. Not so long ago I visited the beautiful little island of Guernsey to follow in the footsteps of Auguste Renoir. The famous French Impressionist painter once made a trip there and painted sixteen or seventeen canvases in just over three weeks. A hundred years later that event was celebrated by the issue of postage stamps showing some of those wonderful masterpieces.

I re-enlisted the help of my friend (of the Yorkshire sheep incident in chapter 2) and off we went in search of Renoir's scenes. My chum is quite brilliant at reading maps. We quickly found our way to Moulin Huet Bay. By studying the stamps, we were able to locate the exact place where I thought the famous artist must have worked. I popped into a handy tea shop set in densely-wooded steep cliffs, and enquired about the illustrious visitor. The charming proprietor turned out to be a Member of Parliament for the island. His family and their ancestors owned the land Renoir visited. The precise spot from where one masterpiece was painted was on their back lawn. The tea was lovely, and the view marvellous. It was another lucky day!

The bay and cliffs were the same as they were in the French painter's day, but you could no longer see them from quite the same angle. Trees had grown and partly obscured the scene down below. We walked down a steep and narrow path to sea level. Maybe Renoir, who was quite old when he made his visit, could not manage this jaunt. I found the bay very interesting. Figure 52 is my drawing of Moulin Huet. It may not be worth quite the same as a Renoir oil (about 24 million

Fig. 52   The bay Renoir painted.

dollars), but 'tis mine own!

Let's examine more closely my drawing of this bay from where Renoir painted several pictures. The heavily-wooded cliff top, you will see, is drawn by dot stipple, lots of it, and it does take time. Again, I purposely added a human figure to give an idea of scale. Just be patient copying this drawing.

Figure 53 is of a huge rock in the same bay. This was one of the subjects featured in Renoir's paintings. For an ink drawing it becomes a useful study of dark and light. I employed dense cross-hatching on the deeply shadowed side of the rock, vertical lines to shade the jagged headland in the distance and small dashes for ripples on the sea. A few patches of seaweed and three gulls were easy to add in order to complete this simple scene. I produced both of these drawings to a small scale with a size 0.1 pen. It will help you if you can make yours twice as big.

Fig. 53   Draw this huge rock.

Mess about with boats

If you love marine pictures you are going to want to draw boats. We shall mess about a bit with them here. Look at those shown in figure 54. The shape of their hulls is always pretty much the same even though there are so many different boat designs.

As the west shore of Guernsey has many natural little harbours formed amongst the jagged reefs, I was able to find a splendid array of types to draw for you.

Notice that masts on sailing boats are never dead centre; they are set forward towards the bow (the sharp end). On bigger yachts there is often a secondary mast near the stern (the blunt end). It will help you to draw a boat accurately if you imagine its hull shape as fitting into a box. Figure 55 illustrates what I mean. This technique is an aid to getting the dreaded perspective right. The canal long boat in figure 56 is an interesting vessel which reveals how its lines must diminish

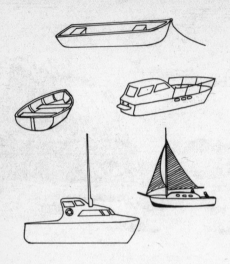

Fig. 54 Different boat designs.

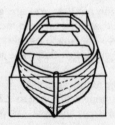

Fig. 55 Box your boat.

(come closer together) as they go back in distance away from you.

Draw all the boats in figures 54, 55 and 56, before going on to figure 57. This is a simple study of a fishing boat on the shore. Fishing boats at rest are one of my favourite subjects. This one should be easy for you to copy.

Fig. 56 Copy this canal boat.

Fig. 57 A fishing boat simply drawn.

The scene in figure 58 is a little more ambitious, but just as straightforward to draw. It shows one of the many natural mini-harbours on Guernsey. I have put in two small wader birds in

Fig. 58 Natural mini-harbours.

the foreground and a contemplative figure at the edge of the sea. The diagonal sky lines suggest space and wind movement. The boat is not slap bang in the middle of the picture. As you will discover in the next chapter, placing it dead-centre would show bad composition. The object of attention is best put to one side so that the drawing is not divided into two. Simple when you know how, isn't it? Copy this example or a similar one.

Quiz
1. Give one good composition point.
2. Where should the main mast of a sailing boat be?
3. Which lines are best used to depict the sea?
4. How can you draw sun reflecting from rocks?

Answers
1. Encourage your viewer to look into your picture.
2. Towards the bow.
3. Short, wavy ones, sometimes of different thicknesses.
4. By using the white paper to show against any shading.

8

BE A GOOD COMPOSER

You may now feel confident enough to tackle drawing from photographs. To be successful you also need to know how to compose a good picture. A camera records things as they are rather than as an artist wants them to be. Most of us become snap-happy when we are on holiday. What looks perfectly lovely through a view-finder often turns out tiny and distant in the resulting snapshot. Somehow it can seem only half the scene you expected. Photographs can nevertheless provide excellent information for a drawing.

As an artist you are free to alter any scene you choose to draw. Two of the greatest English painters changed what they saw in order to produce great works of art. They were John Constable and J.W. Turner. I recall visiting a waterfall in the Yorkshire Dales, specially to see where one magnificent masterpiece had been painted. The painting concerned was done with sparkling golds, yellows and the brilliant use of white and colour to create hazy water-splash and mist. What I found when I got to the force (waterfall) was a let down. The water trickled over a black rock ledge, only to splash down onto more dark rocks. Perhaps the weather had been too dry for too long — but then, I cannot claim Turner's vision or superb technique.

Common faults

Beginner artists tend to ignore composition both through lack of knowledge and the struggle to put down accurate lines. Composition in art refers to the arrangement of things. The most common mistake is to put the horizon far too high up in a drawing. Eye-level in any picture must fall on the imaginery line which lies directly ahead of you when you draw that scene. See Figure 59. You cannot start drawing a landscape seated and stand up half-way through! Eye-level must remain constant.

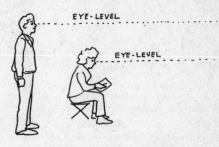

Fig. 59 Different eye-levels.

A low horizon will give an impression of great space and calm. You can easily test how different eye-levels affect pictures. Look at whatever scene is in front of you now. Stand on a chair or bench to look; then sit down and, finally, lie down to look. The latter position is one sometimes used by photographers and artists to give an unusual view point. For most purposes, however, the ideal level for the horizon is about one third of the way up from the bottom edge of a drawing.

Figure 60 illustrates correct and incorrect eye-levels. It also shows another aspect of composition. The two trees in the top drawing are both the same shape and size and are equidistant from you. They therefore divide attention. In the correct version I have balanced one tree against three, placed at different distances. You now see the house as the object of attention.

The next example of a common error is shown in figure 61. The top sketch has a series of horizontal lines, two opposing trees, and a hill in the centre. The lower drawing demonstrates improvements that you can make. Shift the hill off centre, move the trees and rearrange the fields so that the eye is led into the scene. Buy shares in earth-moving equipment!

INCORRECT

CORRECT

Fig. 60 The eye-level is important.

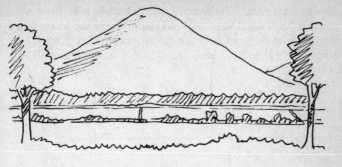

INCORRECT

CORRECT

Fig. 61 Move things.

When learning how to draw landscapes you are tempted to concentrate solely on the items which make up your picture, and to forget about composition. Don't worry! You're in the good company of all who started the same way. Figure 62 shows what I mean. The incorrect sketch has two hills, two trees and two boats which appear to be heading out of the scene. The high horizon does not help this faulty composition. Curiously, odd numbers, 1, 3, 5, etc., are an aid to composition. Now

INCORRECT

CORRECT

Fig. 62 Keep objects in the scene.

INCORRECT

CORRECT

Fig. 63 Stop a river running out of the scene.

study the correct drawing in figure 62. Three boats sail into the picture. Two different size trees are balanced by a broken, rugged shore-line. A lower horizon flattens down the hills,

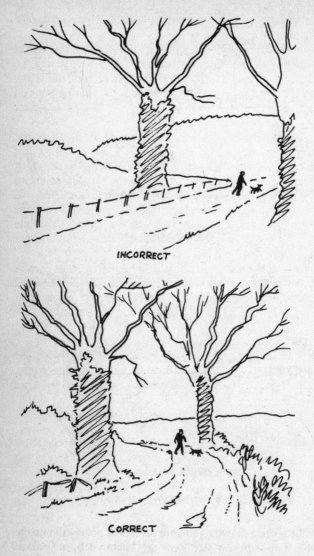

Fig. 64   Balance trees.

and a distant headland has been added. Just a little thought given before *beginning* a drawing can make a huge difference to the finished job.

The faulty composition in figure 63 doesn't seem too bad at first glance but look how much better the correct version is. A raised river bank now prevents the river running out of the picture. A large tree on the right balances the small groups on the left. Eye-level has been brought down to give a greater impression of distance.

Figure 64 is very similar in faults to figure 63. The man and his dog are moving out of the frame. The lane is running off at the edge. One tree dominates the middle of the scene whilst only half of another tree tries to get into the act. The re-drawn example has a winding lane. Its previously uniform fence is now broken down and more interesting. Opposite this fence is now a straggly hedge to add balance. The figures move into the set. The trees have been rearranged and the horizon has been brought down slightly.

You can now see how to compose a good landscape picture from almost any holiday snap or from life. Develop the habit of thinking how *you* want others to see your gem. Make your drawings easy to look at − that's good composition!

Use your freedom

Be uninhibited about changing what you see into what you want to portray. Feel free to chop out, pop in, shift, curve, bend, straighten or whatever. Remember, you are an artist not a camera.

There are exceptions to taking such liberties. For example, you might be commissioned by your millionaire aunt or uncle to draw the ancestral home accurately. Then you would show every cracked window-pane, broken roof tile, dent in the ramparts, and patch of rising damp − or would you?

You can glean a great deal about excellence in composition by visiting a good art gallery and studying the work of old masters. The trick, once you have absorbed what you will − having stood in front of a particular masterpiece − is to remember what your eye *first saw* and then, how you looked around the rest of the painting. Next, have a good think. What had the artist done to make your eye move the way it did? What you discover will give you ideas for your own creations.

A bad composition is one at which people won't waste time looking. Perhaps it is too confusing to the eye; maybe no single item grabs the attention; possibly there are too many conflicting objects.

Quiz
1. What is good composition?
2. Give four composition faults.
3. Why is your eye-level important?
4. What should figures in a landscape be doing?

Answers
1. An arrangement that is easy to look at.
2. Horizon too high. Picture divided. No balance. Figures or such things as rivers or lanes, moving out of the scene.
3. Your eye-level should determine where your horizon is.
4. They should be moving into the picture, or be an integral part of the design.

9

A USEFUL LITTLE AID

A grid is a handy little aid for artists of all abilities. It is easy to make one out of a transparent sheet, marked in squares and sandwiched between two cardboard frames. See figure 66.

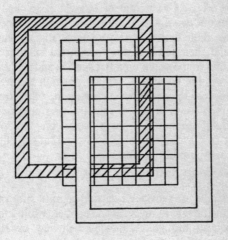

Fig. 66   A grid.

Many famous people in the world of art have used grids. Vincent Van Gogh, for instance, made quite a large one on a stand. He mentioned the gadget in letters to his long-suffering brother who sponsored him throughout his life. Van Gogh used a grid to make a painting of his bed in the asylum at Arles. This picture, which was sold for millions of pounds, is a good example of accurate perspective drawing. Vincent, like me, was a self-taught artist. The comparison ends there — I've no intention of lopping off an ear or shooting myself!

Long before Van Gogh was born artists made grids and used them to study perspective. This artists' tool has been around for a very long time.

How to make a grid

The grid I use was made in half-an-hour from two pieces of scrap cardboard, a sheet of transparent material of the kind used for overhead projectors, and a little glue. The screen is divided into 2cm squares, eight up and the same number across. You can use different measurements or sizes to suit yourself.

Your first job is to mark out squares, in ink, on the transparent sheet. Use a rule or straight edge, and a sharp blade to cut out two identical cardboard frames. These frames should have their external measurements slightly larger than the grid and their internal ones somewhat smaller than the grid. Lay one frame down on a flat surface and put a few dabs of glue along the borders. Carefully position the transparent sheet down onto the cardboard. Prepare the other frame with glue and then lower it down onto the grid so that the two frames stick together. A heavy book on top will hold everything in place until the glue dries. That's all there is to making a very useful drawing aid!

How to use a grid

A grid can be used inside or outside on most subjects. I hold mine at arms' length in my left hand so that, while I am taking frequent squints through it at the object in view, my right hand is free to draw. You can, for example, hold your grid half way to your face in order to view a larger scene. This works well but you must remember for any particular picture always to hold it at the same distance from your eyes and to line it up exactly on the same place each time. For example, on a building, it's best to line up with the corner of a wall or some similar item that you can fairly assume the builder built vertical! Then you can see at once at what angle to draw, say, the gutter line in relation to the horizontal in your picture. Figure 67 will show you what I mean. A grid also helps you draw the right slope on a roof.

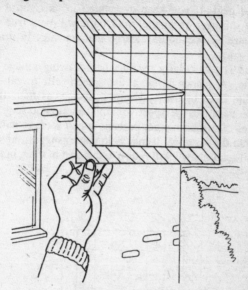

Fig. 67 A useful aid for drawing buildings.

From my simple example above you should be able to appreciate how you will also now be able to use a grid to capture accuracy in lines of perspective to a degree you may never have imagined possible before. The same tool can be used in a slightly modified way as an aid to drawing still-life subjects, trees, hills, humans, and no end of other things. First pencil lightly onto your paper or pad the *same number* of squares you have on your grid. You can then make accurate sketches simply by matching what you draw onto your pad squares to what you see in your grid squares.

If you read my book, *The Right Way to Draw People*, you will remember that a grid can be used to scale a portrait up or down. Provided the number of squares in the grid you place over a portrait is the *same* as the number of squares on your pad it doesn't matter whether those on your pad are larger or smaller; the point is that if, say, the nose, occupies 2½ squares on the portrait grid, then it must fill the same 2½ squares on your pad grid. If you keep everything in its rightful square then, be it bigger or smaller your copy will be a true one. If you wanted to you could enlarge the drawings in this book using a grid.

A grid is particularly useful when drawing village scenes from life. A glance through the screen will reveal exactly where the lines of the buildings converge, as their distance from you increases (perspective). You can use it to see just how the edges of a road merge, perhaps round a curve and out of sight, into the distance. It may help you to suggest the camber of a road accurately. I will return to this sort of thing in the next chapter.

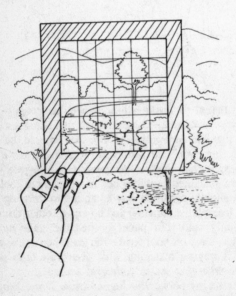

Fig. 68   A grid helps with composition.

Help with landscapes

Looking through a grid will help you decide what to leave in or take out of a landscape. In other words, how to improve your composition. Study figure 68.

Beginner artists faced with a vast spectacular panorama which covers scores of miles often try to cram the lot onto a small A5 sketch pad! This is a common mistake which use of a grid will prevent. The picture to be drawn in my figure 68, for example, is that part in the frame.

If you want to draw a wide landscape, and there's no reason why you shouldn't, you could still use a grid, but it would have to be wide enough to cover the scene. This entails making a much bigger screen. I pesonally don't think it's worth carting around more than one small grid. Frequent use of this will teach you quickly what to look for, and what to draw. You will gain the experience to tackle panoramic scenes with suitably huge confidence and enthusiasm without the need for a giant grid.

Quiz

1. Why use a grid?
2. How does a grid help you?
3. What is a grid useful for?

Answers

1. It will improve your drawing.
2. It enables you to get things in their rightful place.
3. You name it!

10

DOWN IN THE VILLAGE

Your grid will be useful for copying drawings in this chapter. We're going down to the village to see what stirs. Ancient hamlets and villages are part of England's rich heritage. They are attractive features of our land, and have particular appeal for many city dwellers. Each village has its own character and architecture.

The village of Dent in the Yorkshire Dales is a clean, charming example which many artists have drawn. There is a nice tea room there — for what more could one ask? Figure 70 is my sketch of part of this lovely place. These cottages are overlooked by high fells. The roofs are made of hand-cut rock slabs which are very heavy. Those at the bottom of the roof are larger than the ones at the top. In the left foreground bright red tulips were in contrast with smart yellow specimens in the back rows.

My friend and I stopped here to draw this scene. Many of the walkers passing through paused to exchange a cheerful word or have a peep at our efforts. It's nice being an artist!

My ink illustration was produced on a small pad with a size 0.1 pen. I kept the scene as simple as possible. I preferred shading to denote strong shadow, rather than blocking in too heavily. Study the basic construction lines in figure 71 before starting your own copy. Get these right and the result is straightforward. The grid from the previous chapter will be handy for this. It's wise to use a pencil for the first rough draft. I use a straight edge to get the vertical lines correct, but ink them in freehand. You might try this method. To rule lines

Fig. 70 Part of a lovely village.

directly with a pen makes the drawing appear much too clean cut. The hand made stones and slabs are not perfectly square or straight anyway.

Move about your village

You will find it useful to wander all around a village before you choose your precise subject. Different vantage points can dramatically alter the possibilities for a drawing.

Another part of Dent is shown in figure 72. The near cottage had a rounded corner wall. I suggested the cobbled street by drawing patches of elliptical marks and small dashes. I didn't attempt to cover all the ground in the same way, which would probably have made the finished picture too dark. The houses here, compared to those in a city, are quite small. See how my building stones are drawn. Some I have hatched diagonally.

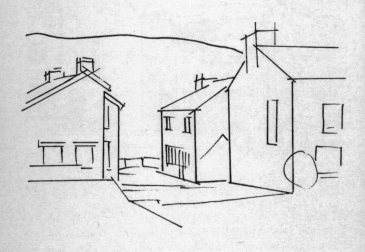

Fig. 71   Draw these lines accurately.

Fig. 72   A corner of Dent.

Others I have marked with curved dashes. Then, where I
wanted shadow, I have loosely cross-hatched over the top of the
sketched stones. Figure 73 shows how I did this. I put in the
lady to give interest and show scale. I have drawn her slightly
larger in figure 74 to help you see her proportions. If you can
get her basic shape right then she's easy to draw.

One tiny village of this beauty can contain enough scenes to
keep you busy for days. Figure 75 illustrates next what Dent

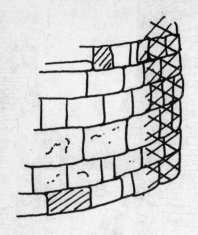

Fig. 73 How the shadow is recorded.

Fig. 74 Get the basic shape right.

Fig. 75 Another street in Dent.

Main Street looks like from an approach road. The houses on
the left are white-washed as is the one which forms the
background to a massive rock set on the corner of Main Street.
This rock is a memorial to Adam Sedgwick, 1785–1873. He
was a local boy who made good and became a notable scholar
and benefactor to the village.

Fig. 76   Keep figures simple.

The wide variety of buildings in Dent makes it a more than usually interesting place. The ancient hand-cut rocks in figure 75 are nice to draw. The white-walled cottages are easy to sketch. The cobbled streets, with a line of single stones marking the gutter, must be pretty much the same today as when they were first laid down. Notice in figure 75 how I used fine cross-hatching for deep shadows. Putting in the people helped to create an impression of distance. They were treated simply. Have a look at figure 76 before sketching them.

Draw the basic shapes of the buildings in pencil, then, when you are satisfied, ink them in. I can recommend this delightful place — and the pot of Yorkshire tea that we drank there!

A bird's-eye view

When I stayed in Bourton-on-the-Water, in the Cotswolds, I had a wonderful bird's-eye view of the buildings standing opposite to the one I was in. I decided to draw the view as it was, rather than to shift some of the trees away. Figure 77 — the result — was sketched quite small on an A5 pad. I used a 0.5 pen to do a controlled scribble with lots of dots for the trees, but switched to a size 0.1 pen for the buildings.

Roof-top scenes can make attractive drawings. I have seen many over the years. London, Paris, Venice and other cities provide the roof-top artist with endless choice. You might like

Fig. 77   A bird's-eye view.

to try some of your own — but be careful how you scramble about high up to gain the best view! It may be safer for you to start off by copying figure 77.

Round a corner

To wander round an unknown corner and discover a pleasant scene is always a nice surprise. The picture I drew for figure 78 is a good example of this. It also shows how perspective is used. Notice the way lines converge as they recede from you, and how there is a subtle change to that as the road bends round in the distance. This place was just a few minutes' walk from where I stayed at Bourton-on-the-Water. There had been a sudden rain storm which left pools of water along the gutters. This, from an artistic point of view, was helpful as I was able to fill in areas of road to suggest the floods. A mass of pink, red, purple and white flowers hung from the near wall and gave natural balance to the houses opposite. I first drew the guide lines in pencil as in figure 79.

The near wall, where I stood, I sketched with a size 0.1 pen. The mortar used between the Cotswold stones was in quite thick layers. Look how I took in the details. I switched to a size 0.5 pen to illustrate the hanging flowers using a controlled scribble and many dots. The small scale of this illustration did not allow for much fine detail of window frames and panes to be drawn. So, I simplified the nearest ones and, for the cottages furthest into the picture, reduced the detail even more.

See how many dots I had to use to suggest not just the stone material of these buildings, but also to bring out the "tide" mark made by rain over the years. I employed dots again to

Fig. 78   Fine lines and many dots.

Fig. 79 Draw in pencil first.

show lichen on the roofs. Finally I popped a small figure of a man in on the far bend. Copy this picture. It could be one to be proud of.

Quiz
1. How are vertical building lines best drawn?
2. You walk into a village ready to be quick on the draw; what should you do first?
3. Why use human figures in a composition?
4. Which pen technique is especially useful for village scenes?

Answers
1. With a straight edge and pencil followed by inking in freehand.
2. Walk around and take a good *look*. Your first vantage point may not be the best (or serve the best tea!).
3. To give an idea of scale and distance.
4. The good old dot and dash.

11

HAPPY CHRISTMAS!

It could well be the height of spring or summer when you read this chapter, but never mind! What is important is that you now have enough skill to produce your own Christmas cards for the forthcoming year. What would be nicer to send to special relatives and friends!

Millions of greetings cards sell each year and Christmas card sales often set new records. Interestingly, however, snow scenes in black and white, which are the main subject of this chapter, are comparatively rare. They have their own charm and are easy to draw. People really appreciate a hand-drawn and made card. You have had practice sketching trees, buildings and landscapes so the exercises that follow are, perhaps, the most simple to draw in this book!

Design your own bestseller

Christmas cards fall into a relatively few common design categories, easy to discern if you look through ones you have received over the years. Doing so will swiftly enable you to sketch out possible designs for your own Christmas cards. Remember that all *published* designs are covered by copyright law and must not be copied. Ideas have no such protection. You can take your own village scenes, cottages, churches, or whatever, and fit them into your own composition, albeit a similar one to many others used by scores of artists over the years.

The robin, by the way, is Britain's favourite bird. It is featured on thousands of cards. It may be sitting on a fencepost, a snow-covered branch, a spade handle, or be portrayed as a chirpy cartoon. So whilst we concentrate upon landscapes we shall allow the brave robin his place just for fun.

Materials needed

Excellent greetings cards can be made from good quality cartridge drawing paper or white card. The cost is comparatively low. You already have the pens, pencils, and a rule. You will need a pointed tool, such as a metal knitting needle, or an awl; then you are ready to start your mini-production unit.

The right size

A Christmas card can be portrait or landscape in format as shown in figure 80. Some are square, but to suit these pages we shall work on the above mentioned shapes.

You should first decide what size of *envelope* you will use. This sounds obvious doesn't it? It wasn't for me in my early days. I churned out several dozen cards only to find that they were bigger than the envelopes I had bought! We all make mistakes don't we? Make your cards slightly smaller than the type of envelope you choose.

Be sure to draw your design on the *front* cover and the right way up. This also seems obvious. I once drew several illustrations on the back. There's one born every minute, isn't there?

Cut your blank card with a sharp blade or guillotine. You then mark a middle line and gently score down this with the aid of a rule and a pointed stick, metal knitting needle or an awl. See figure 81. Your card will then fold cleanly.

Start with a rough

It is wise first to draw your chosen design in *pencil* on thin typing or tracing paper. This is called a rough. When you are satisfied with your sketch you transfer it onto your card. You do so by first rubbing a soft pencil over the main lines of your picture but on the *back* of your paper. Then, to transfer this onto the front cover of your card, just position your rough right-way-up exactly over the front of your card where you

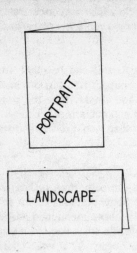

Fig. 80   Two types of card design.

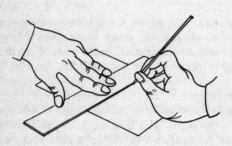

Fig. 81   Score with a pointed stick or knitting needle or awl. Then fold the blank card.

want it to be and go over the design with a Biro or pointed hard pencil. This operation is quite quick to do and produces your good drawing directly onto the card ready for you to ink in.

Study figure 82 for an easy example to begin with. The snow-filled sky is suggested by horizontal lines which are best done fast with a delicate, loose grip that simply skims across the surface of the paper. Many beginners tend to make these lines too slowly and with too much pressure on the pen. This results in thick, laboured lines.

Dense cross-hatching for the hawthorns behind the cottages was deliberately darkened to emphasise the snow-covered roofs. A trick-of-the-trade I'm happy to share with you! The shrubs beyond the posts in the foreground help to bring the picture forward.

The robin has little detail. You could leave him out without affecting the general design, but the bird does help to give a touch of Christmas. My card was finished off by putting a double border round it. This can be done with a red or blue pen.

I prefer to put a greeting or good wishes caption inside my cards, but these are equally effective on the top or bottom of a drawing. The choice is yours. You might care to experiment in pencil before deciding.

A church features in figure 83. This scene is very easy to draw and quite effective as a winter picture. The large tree and buildings were first lightly drawn in pencil. Then the sky lines were put in. These go round distant snow-covered hills. A winding lane leads into the picture and overtakes two human figures who trudge through the snow. Notice the way shading has been used on the buildings, and how the cross-hatched trees behind the church help to bring things forward. Far away hedgerows are shown by simple vertical shading, and three fence posts lead into the scene. The big tree is shaded with fine hatching. Darkened areas again highlight the snow-packed roofs. An easy one for you to copy. Get busy!

The landscape shaped wintry scene in figure 84 is another easy-to-draw card for you to try. The frozen river is depicted by thin horizontal lines – another fast skim job. The cottage, trees and distant forest are all easily sketched. This one might

Fig. 82   Draw a Christmas robin.

Fig. 83 This is simple to draw.

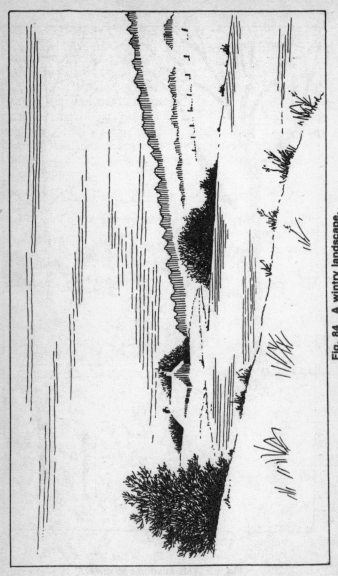

Fig. 84 A wintry landscape.

be sent to your bank manager. Off you go!

Happy everything

Christmas cards, of course, are not the only greetings cards produced. Easter and Valentine cards have tremendous sales. There are also ever-increasing sales of many others: Mother's, Father's, Granny's, Grandad's, Get-well, Get lost, and a host more jostle for attention as each big day approaches. You can now use your artistic ability to make your own little marvels for private consumption. Don't be nervous about advertising your skill, using your humour, or showing your affection for someone special. It's all good fun.

Quiz

1. What is the first problem with card making?
2. How could you go wrong?
3. What technique is best for drawing sky lines?
4. What is an important consideration with your card?

Answers

1. The card must fit the envelope.
2. By using the wrong side or size.
3. Skimming your pen quickly across the paper.
4. It must be easy to look at. It must please the receiver.

12

ADVANCE AND BE RECOGNISED

Now that you can draw pretty well it's time to advance and be recognised as an artist. Well done! You will have no new problems with copying the slightly harder examples in the following pages. All you need is patience and a bit of time.

Before writing this book I had never been to Northumberland. Now, I'm happy to report, this wonderful county of northern England has been roamed in order to draw some of the illustrations in this chapter. Figure 86 is the first of these. When I looked back at this little valley I saw that it had a natural composition, and was easy to sketch. It is the sort of scene that is fine for a greetings card.

Note the way the dry stone wall follows the contours of the slopes. The shadow cast by the tree in the centre also helps to suggest the form of the land. The line of fence posts does the same. A line of tough, spiky grass marks the course of a dried-up stream. The clouds were first put in with pencil then the horizontal sky lines were inked up to these outlines. This is the best way of depicting clouds. I used a size 0.1 pen. Distant fells are recorded by light, broken lines. Shrubs and trees have been drawn with dot stipple. This drawing could be one to keep for yourself or pass to the fell-walker in your family.

I joined a cheerful group of walkers, who had six Canadians with them, to ramble along the lovely coastal stretches. The weather was great for walking and the views were lovely. Figure 87 shows a small harbour that we came across. It seemed to be waiting for an artist to sketch! The humans gave

Fig. 86   A little valley with natural composition.

it interest. The sea was fairly calm except for a few ripples near a deep shelf at the edge of the shore. The harbour walls were constructed of natural rock but were also faced with concrete slabs in places. I drew the dense shadows in the water with a

Fig. 87   A harbour in a fishing village in Northumberland.

controlled scribble which tapered off into diagonal strokes to show ripples. Deep shade on the near wall was obtained with normal cross-hatching. You should have no trouble with this one.

The Duke's estate

One of the nicest walks I did was through the well-kept estate of the Duke of Northumberland. I didn't meet the Duke or find a tea room but the marvellous scenes made up for this. Figure 88 is an illustration of a lane on the estate. It is really a study of simple shading and dot stipple which you will manage easily.

A famous spot on the estate is the hermit's cave. It has outside a statue of the late tenant — whom I named Kermit! Figure 89 is my drawing of this interesting scene. It's not really a landscape but I thought it would be a good exercise for you to do. Kermit the hermit lived in this cave several hundred years ago. It may have been the "in thing" for Dukes to keep a tame hermit. The tough old boy, I was told, hung about the estate for eight years. The cave is quite large inside, but very draughty and damp. Kermit has lost one hand. I don't know what book he is reading but it's not one of mine! He must have been a remarkable chap to have a sculpture made in his honour.

I drew this picture first in pencil. Then I began the finished picture by inking in the cave with a small brush and drawing ink. The dark coloured leafy moss above the cave I did with a controlled scribble. I used dots and dashes with a size 0.5 pen to show beech masts scattered around the entrance. The rock ledge, just inside the cave opening, I cross-hatched to create depth and suggest deep shadow. That is all there is to producing this unusual illustration. Give it a go.

Figure 90 shows an extended landscape as seen from a high point on the Duke's estate. What a super back garden! This is a straightforward example for you to copy. I used simple cross-hatching to show afforested areas in the middle distance and the foreground. While this technique might not seem to be wholly realistic it does give an accurate effect of tone (depth of colour or shade). Very often the simple way proves to be the best one. Notice how an impression of distance is created by

Fig. 88   A lane on the Duke's estate.

Fig. 89 The hermit's cave.

the diminishing size of the fields and trees. Copy this drawing with your finest size pen.

A castle in the air

Another coastal walk took me to a castle in the air. Lindisfarne Castle, in figure 91, is perched on a pinnacle of rugged rock that juts through folds of grass. I drew the rock with a kind of controlled scribble made up of squiggly lines and then shaded them over where the shadows were. You could get "writer's" cramp putting in all the dot stipple in this example! I saw many visitors when I was there but just drew two of them to give an idea of scale. While working on this sketch I also had the pleasure of drawing baby rabbits which popped out within a pace of where I was. They seemed interested in what I was doing!

Fig. 90 This would be a nice back garden.

Fig. 91 Lindisfarne Castle.

A few miles out to sea from this castle are the Farne Islands. They are well worth a visit to see thousands of sea birds. There are also hundreds of sleepy looking Atlantic seals who seem untroubled by scores of snap-happy tourists.

A drop of Scottish water

Figure 92, a waterfall in bonnie Scotland, is the last drawing in this chapter for you to copy. See how dense cross-hatching

Fig. 92   A Scottish waterfall.

on rocks helps to emphasise water. Light areas left blank in the water suggest the foaming rush of it cascading down the rocks. Note how shading shows through the tree on the right of the scene. This is an easy drawing but it does take time. I'm sure you will manage it.

Quiz
1. What was difficult to draw in this chapter?
2. What items suggest land form?
3. What is tone?
4. Which technique is often the best one to use?

Answers
1. Not a thing!
2. Shadow, fences, walls, trees.
3. Depth of colour or shade.
4. The simplest way.

13

PERSPECTIVE WITHOUT FEAR

Perspective, as I have tried to show you, can be learned naturally by discovering how to *look*. Experience leads to knowing whether a sketch is right or wrong. A grid, as seen in chapter 9, can be a great aid too. In this chapter, however, I shall explain the theory of perspective. Now that you have gained so much practice it should make much more sense to you.

A vanishing point

Imagine that you are standing on a hill. You look across a perfectly flat plain which is divided by perfectly square tree-lined fields. Figure 93 shows this unlikely scene. Your eye-level is the distant horizontal line. The spot at which *all* "going away" dividing lines converge is called the vanishing point. I have marked this with a cross. You can see what happens to these lines and how this affects the crossing lines. Although we know these are square fields they are not drawn square; to make the picture look correct they each have to diminish towards your eye-level. This is a very basic way of understanding perspective. That wasn't so bad was it?

We usually become more aware of perspective when we start to draw a building. Figure 94 shows how perspective applies to a row of houses which are to the right of the viewer. I have simplified this drawing of a village named Dallington, which is in Northamptonshire, so that you can concentrate on the perspective.

I stood on a footbridge so that the buildings were to my right, and my eye-level and the vanishing point (x) were straight

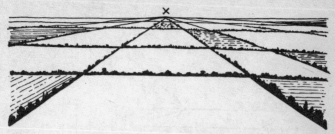

Fig. 93 X marks the vanishing point.

ahead. See how straight lines, if extended from the window-ledges, roofs, chimneys, pavement and stream before they take a curve to the right, would all converge at the vanishing point. The bend in the stream beyond the bridge means that its lines do not follow the others all the way. This is a simple example. The one in figure 95 shows what happens when one or more buildings are different from those they adjoin. The end house here, an inn in Dallington, has a steeply pitched roof. The perspective lines from this roof reach your eye-level slightly away from the place that the perspective lines from the other buildings meet. So it's possible to have more than one vanishing point in the same picture. You could have a scene that contains one row of houses on the left, one on the right and another, off-set from these, towards the centre of the picture. In this event you just work away at each set of lines in each separate group. Note that a vanishing point can itself vanish! It can be off your picture to either side.

Perspective applies to all things

I'm sure that you are wise enough to know that perspective applies to all things seen and drawn. It makes no difference whether your subject is indoors or up a mountain. Photographs clearly show perspective. You can see it in straight roads, lanes, canals, and so on. However, beginners still tend to be confused. Perhaps the dreaded word itself puts them into shock! Whatever it may be, it remains common for budding artists not to know quite how to handle perspective.

EYE LEVEL

Fig. 94   How perspective works.

The answer for you (as for all!) is simple. First put in your eye-level. Then remember that all perspective lines run to there. Figure 96 illustrates how two rows of trees here (they could be a row of houses) have *two* vanishing points along the same eye-level. It doesn't matter that the trees in either row may be different heights or shapes, the vanishing point stays the same for all the trees in each row. *When you sit and draw, your eye-level remains constant.* It follows that all the vanishing points you need will always be *on this same line.* Newcomers go wrong here — their eye-level moves about. In reality this only happens if you hop up and down!

Don't let perspective bother you. In most general landscape drawing you will manage fine with pen, pencil, grid and your own good eyes. If you like sketching buildings, and many do, then what you have just read will help you to produce correct work.

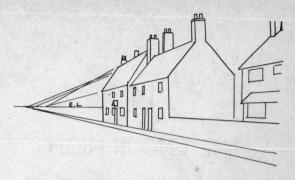

Fig. 95 Different roofs give different lines.

Fig. 96 Two vanishing points on the same eye-level.

Quiz
1. What can give you help with perspectives?
2. What is a vanishing point?
3. Do all lines meet at the same point?
4. Does your eye-level stay the same?

Answers
1. Pen, pencil, grid, a good *look*. Knowing the theory.
2. A spot on the eye-level where lines converge.
3. No.
4. Yes, provided you don't move.

14

THE END IS NIGH

You have almost finished this course and now have enough talent, experience and technique to tackle any landscape on earth. It would be a good idea to put the date on each of your drawings. When you look back you can then see what progress you have made.

Drawing is good for you
Many of my students have found and commented that learning to draw is therapeutic. They are right. You tend not to worry about other problems when you enjoy learning or practising a skill. I became aware of this on a recent visit to the far eastern fells in the English Lake District, when I stopped to sketch a stone circle. I felt lucky and happy. I love wild, remote Moor Divock, near the village of Helton. A favourite bird of mine, the curlew, provided a background of magical calls. The ancient monument, constructed by an early tribe, is featured in figure 97. Notice how the distant hills are cloaked with cloud shadow. You may care to copy this drawing.

Lake Ullswater is not far away from this stone circle. I did a fast ink sketch of the scene from the Glenridding end of the lake, looking away from the water. Heavy rain was imminent. I shaded the mountains simply, to show how distant hills appeared dense in tone and others became lighter towards the foreground. Figure 98 shows this. Try making a quick copy.

Another moor that I have walked is Knipe Moor which is a mile or two from Bampton village. The illustration shown in figure 99 is of a farm which is marked on maps as Howgate

Fig. 97 Stone circle, Moor Divock.

Foot. It nestled in a valley well below my level at the time. It was an interesting and unusual view. This drawing is full of dot stipple. It took around an hour to do. See how long you take on it. It would help you to draw first in pencil the buildings, the walls, and the cow in the back garden.

A history lesson as well

It sometimes happens that a history lesson comes your way when you are out drawing. I walked with a group of ramblers up Glen Coe in the west highlands of Scotland. We came to forbidding looking mountains which, I discovered, marked the

Fig. 98   A view from Lake Ullswater.

site of the massacre back in 1692. During that time the
Macdonald clan lived in scattered stone cottages and farms in
the area. It was their custom to treat all strangers to a free meal
and lodgings for the night. The Campbell clan invaded their
land and took advantage of the Macdonald's hospitality. During
a cold, dark night the Campbells went on to use their hosts for
sword practice, or else knocked in their heads. A few
Macdonalds escaped into the grim hills. I offer no marks for
guessing to which clan the person telling me this story
belonged!

Figure 100 is my sketch of Glen Coe. This is an easy one for
you to copy with a size 0.1 pen.

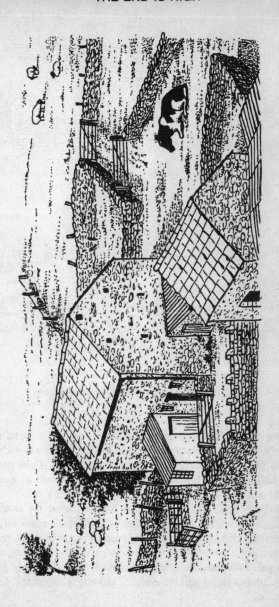

Fig. 99 Howgate Foot farm.

Fig. 100   Scene of a grim event, Glen Coe.

Venture forth

Now it's time for you to venture forth and prove to all that you are an artist. You may not have to go far. Figure 101 is a sketch which I made of a scene from one of my local parks. The long shadows interested me. You could find a similar picture waiting to be drawn near to where you live.

You will need the right clothes and footwear for outdoor work. A hat with a brim or peak is a must — especially in bright light. When it's cold a hat helps to retain body warmth. Waterproofs are a good idea. You can carry your drawing gear in a small rucksack, travel bag or case. A folding stool or foam plastic mat to sit on will be useful. Take enough food and drink

Fig. 101   A park sketch.

to sustain you — important if there isn't a tea room handy. If you take along this book you need never be stuck for information about what technique to use. Good luck!

More Paperfronts by Mark Linley

THE RIGHT WAY TO DRAW

Anyone can learn to draw. But doing so with confidence only comes quickly if you get the basics right.

Mark Linley explains the principles to you, step-by-step, just as if he were teaching you personally during one of his many art classes.

See how easy it is to draw people, animals, trees, buildings, views and still life.

THE RIGHT WAY TO DRAW PEOPLE

Mark Linley shows how drawing people can be fun! First, he helps you map the outlines for the complete form. Next, he teaches you how the shape of the head, the body, the arms and the legs, all flow into that form, in proportion, before any detail is added. Then, you advance in easy-to-follow steps that bring all the features *alive*.

Within moments of opening this book, you will be drawing people, and amazing yourself and friends with your success!

Uniform with this book

FREE